THE GIVEN AND THE CHOSEN

THE GIVEN AND THE CHOSEN

ANN LAUTERBACH

OMNIDAWN PUBLISHING

RICHMOND, CALIFORNIA

2011

Sections 6, 7, and 10 from the poem "Of Being Numerous" by George Oppen,
from NEW COLLECTED POEMS, copyright ©1968 by George Oppen
are reprinted by permission of New Directions Publishing Corp.

Cover photo by Ann Lauterbach
Cover and Interior Design by Cassandra Smith

Typefaces: Warnock Pro and Waters Titling Pro

Printed on 50# Glatfelter Offset B18 Eggshell

Library of Congress Cataloging-in-Publication Data

Lauterbach, Ann, 1942-
The given and the chosen / Ann Lauterbach.
p. cm.
ISBN 978-1-890650-62-9 (pbk. : alk. paper)
I. Title.
PS3562.A844G58 2011
811'.54--dc23
2011036805

Published by Omnidawn Publishing, Richmond, California
www.omnidawn.com   (510) 237-5472   (800) 792-4957
10 9 8 7 6 5 4 3 2 1
ISBN: 978-1-890650-62-9

to Marina van Zuylen and Stephan Wolohojian

The abiding struggle of art is then to convert materials that are stammering and dumb in ordinary experience into eloquent media.

John Dewey, *Art as Experience*

The eye on each wing, for example,
many have mentioned this.

That it sees nothing,
no one has mentioned this.

Michael Palmer, "Finisterrae"

A FEW DAYS AGO I was having dinner with a friend, the novelist Paul La Farge, and he asked: what is this talk you are giving at SVA about? The description is mysterious. Maybe he said *unclear*, maybe he said *ambiguous*. Ah, I thought, that again. The *about*. It's an old question, the subject of the subject. People ask, when I tell them I am a poet, "what are your poems about?" It is a question I can almost never answer. The poems find their subjects as they are made. I do not want to suggest that there is no there there, no outside. On the contrary, the world, its objects and events, press toward the poems, competing for a place, and I have to try to make sufficient room for this crowd, this variousness. But the world as such cannot be in the poem, only language can be in the poem. Language is the poem's material given. I might then say, in answer to the question, what are your poems about, what is this talk about, that they are about what might arise between the given and the chosen.[1]

I THINK THAT THE art and writing I most care about thickens and eludes, blurs and enriches, my sense of the subject, so that who I am and what it is engage in a fluid exchange. This is not a mystical experience; one does not depart into some other realm; it is instead an intensification of the awareness of consciousness itself. The mediate space between Freud's pleasure principle and the death drive, Eros and Thanatos, is this third term, the will to make something from something: poesis. Eros moves us toward the other, desiring, and Thanatos pushes back with the limit, the end. Between the two, forms occur.

MY SENSE OF PLEASURE, both as a writer and as a viewer or reader, derives in part from feeling at the indeterminate threshold, the shift, between the given and the chosen.

Wallace Stevens: *Notes toward a Supreme Fiction*

> *He had to choose. But it was not a choice*
> *Between excluding things. It was not a choice*

Between, but of. He chose to include the things
That in each other are included, the whole,
The complicate, the amassing harmony.[2]

THE GIVEN AND THE CHOSEN. The gift and the choice.
The prior and the yet to come. The two terms do not form
a proper binary; they do not glare at each other over an
abyss of opposition or negation, but rather slide toward
and away from each other like sunlight on a wire. They
seem to carry spiritual or even religious overtones, with
phrases like the *gift of life* and the *chosen people* hovering
uneasily over our secular heads. There is an unnerving
temporal ambiguity between the fact of the given and
the incipience of the gift, between the apprehension of
more than one and the preferential, limiting, moment of
choice. Etymologically, choice gathers to itself taste and
wish and favor, enjoyment, desire, love and pleasure. Gift,
on the other hand, brings with it payment, specifically for
a wife, and poison. But those of you who are familiar with
the work of Marcel Mauss or Lewis Hyde[3] know that the
concept of the gift is both ancient and vexed, touching at
the very quick of our notions of reciprocity and exchange,

as well as our sense of what is innate. The child, we say, is gifted.

I LIVE NOW IN THE COUNTRY, and am increasingly conscious of the dispositions of choice in relation to time, the temporal economy of being. Many of us, persons whose lives are reasonably successful and who have a fairly normal complement of responsibilities, seem to live perpetually close of a kind of temporal anarchy. Days are spent in stressed imbalances between needs and desires, preparations and accomplishments, the wish for solitude and the wish to participate. Expectation and result, effort and efficacy, reception and response, these permutating causalities feel attenuated, torn. It is as if we were suspended like atomic particles in a hectic medium, each unable to either come to rest or to find our way to the solace of molecular attachments. Our hope that the heart and mind will work in concert, and that this heartmind will be embodied in our actions and responses, seems as near as a walk on the beach in February. For our time, perhaps Michel Foucault came closest to diagnosing the causes of anguish for the modern Western subject. Deleuze, speaking about Foucault, remarks, "Finally, in the last books, there's the discovery of thought as . . . establishing ways of existing or, as Nietzsche put it, inventing new possibilities of life. Existing not as a subject but as a work of art—and this last phase presents thought as artistry."[4]

MANY YEARS AGO, it might have been 1973 or 1974, I gave a course at Saint Martins School of Art in London called "choice, decision, and judgment." I was interested then, as I am now, in asking questions about the possible relation between forms of life and forms of art. At the time, I was concerned with individuals, persons, identities; I wanted to know if the sequence of choice, decision, and judgment in one's quotidian life might have some bearing on that same sequence, choice, decision, judgment, in making art. Was there some innate tendency or even habit in both domains that could be discerned, so that a work of art somehow captured the essence of a person? Contrarily, could the process of making choices, decisions and judgments in art-making in fact condition and shape a person's life? Perhaps unsurprisingly, the figure that came closest to resolving this conundrum for me was John Cage. In Cage there seemed to be a continuum between the given and the chosen so closely calibrated as to be indistinguishable, seamless. One sensed in Cage an active receptivity that reconfigured desire into a form of waiting or listening; that reset choice into operations of chance. Somehow Cage had found a way to convert life into art and art into life; this seemed to me an emblem of personal contentment that might extend into the world as an ethical proposal.[5]

I GREW UP in lower Manhattan,[6] the child of urban enlightened secular progressive left idealists steeped in utopian visions of the possibility of making a better world. One of them, my father, would die of polio when he was thirty-six, and the other, my mother, would become an alcoholic and abandon her children, dying at fifty-three. Perhaps it is the dissonance between these initial sets that made me curious in the first place to think about the relation of the given to the chosen.

I FIND MYSELF aware of a residuum that settles down below fluxual reality, beneath all attempts to change or reconfigure the facts and their consequences into fresh potentials. This residuum is like a flavor, a stain or a scent in the sense that these things can stay behind after the agent has left. What is the nature of this residuum in terms of subjective experience? In my case it is a combination of precariousness and loss as initial, given, tropes of existence. These feelings govern the various ameliorations of a somewhat productive life; they cannot be dislodged. But neither need they orchestrate the animate attachments to the actual that beckon, engage, and enhance the days. The self, I want to believe, is layered and aspectual: it can shift and turn and connect variously to various stimuli; it has agility at its core, a mechanism of survival and response which can be freed from ingrained habit. Habits are economical for sure, but they cost us in fluidity, openness, quickness. How, then, do we integrate our sense of self with our will to change?

SITTING IN MY LIVING ROOM with my friend and former student, poet and translator Stacy Doris. We are having an easy conversation, which comes into focus when she comments that we all have an inheritance—language, family, culture, generation—but that what we do is to "take this responsibility and reconfigure it." These words "responsibility" and "reconfigure" are precise in relation to my concerns about subjectivity and art-making. I like the idea that certain givens, or inheritances, which cannot be factually altered, can be "reconfigured" sometimes beyond all recognition. This reconfiguration does not abandon the initial, individuated reality but alters its internal shape, its syntax if you will, to allow new possibilities. The fact of the reconfiguration provides an opening through which what already exists finds itself in what does not yet exist. This opening is an invitation.

BY NOW IT MUST BE CLEAR TO YOU that I am disinclined to the force of linear argument, wary of the discretions of causal logic. Not surprisingly, I am also fearful of authority and certitude. I like to assemble pieces, fragments, stuff, I like to digress and wander and scan, in the hopes of making an arrangement of suggestive, provisional affiliations. The idea is to leave enough room for others, for other subjectivities, to engage and explore, as if they were guests. We do not ask guests to strip themselves of their stuff when they come into our dwellings—at least not yet. We are hoping to provide a place for animated conversation, in which gaps and silences, shifts in tone, curiosity and inquiry, might be accommodated; in which our interpretations and responses are safe. Hospitality opens out toward the circulations of the commons, the public social space now all but lost in the slippages of scroll and screen and cell.

IS IT ALREADY A GIVEN, a truism, a cliché of the contemporary: that the artificial tissue of access provided by the Internet has made us feel less connected, more abstract and estranged from each other and from the world? Is it also already a truism that to question or resist this new habitat is either reactionary or futile, or both?

Cassandra is waiting in the wings.

SOME NOTES HASTILY SCRIBBLED while watching the *NewsHour* with Jim Lehrer on PBS, 4 January 2010. Three technology experts have been asked to assess the next decade: "part of the conversation" "harder to consume?" "everyone is a creator" "throw-away" "libertarian paternalism" "people want to be led" "a tool, not an obligation" "media shift" "we're all watching each other" "vaster wasteland" "shake in, rather than shake out" "not enough jobs" "fading industry" "frivolous, for free" "not institutions but individuals with things to do" "arrival of sensors" "observe and manipulate" "robot revolution" "avatar."

IN 1908 THE GERMAN SOCIOLOGIST Georg Simmel wrote about the abiding question of the difference between nature and culture. "Culture" he wrote, "exists only if man draws into his development *something that is external to him*. Cultivation is certainly a state of the soul, but one that is reached only by means of the use of purposely created *objects*."[7] But for Simmel, the technological objects of modernity, artifacts of human imagination and ingenuity, were becoming increasingly autonomous; controlled, as he put it, by an "internal logic tied to their instrumentality," unable to be absorbed, to add to cultural experience. As the Futurists embraced the iconic turbines of a mechanized utopia, as Malevich and Kandinsky explored the ravishing geometries of an abstract, visionary landscape, the instrumental logic of brute indifference was also being born. Modernity, nothing if not enraptured by the rabid calculations of the new, seems to have barely noticed that the new by its very nature would consume and be consumed.

I DID NOT CATCH the names of the three techno-gurus

on the *NewsHour*, but not long afterwards I saw a review of a book in the *Times*, and the author's photo was of one of them, Jaron Lanier. Lanier's book is called *You are Not a Gadget: A Manifesto*. Lanier, who was born in 1960, and was an early participant in the dot.com revolution, credited with the formulation "virtual reality," sets out a series of fragmentary perceptions and comments from, as it were, inside the game. He speaks about "cybernetic totalism." He says, "Information is alienated experience." He says that the ideology of the digital world has failed both spiritually and behaviorally. The spiritual failure denies what he calls "the mystery of the existence of experience." The behavioral failure involves what he calls "the ubiquitous invocations of anonymity and crowd identity." The utopian vision of a "free and open" culture that might turn toward economic benefits for many, if not all, has also failed. The middle class continues to dwindle; wealth continues to concentrate. "If we can't formulate digital ideals before our appointment with destiny," he warns, "we will have failed to bring about a better world. Instead, we will usher in a dark age in which everything human is devalued."[8]

MANIFESTOES BY NATURE are given to exaggeration

and hyperbole, but Lanier stirs up free-floating anxiety. What we assume as given—our humanity—might be being taken away, eradicated, annulled before our very eyes. We have heard such alarms before. Ortega Y Gasset,[9] in 1948, thought that abstraction was dehumanizing art; television was seen as the death of familial conversation and literacy. It is hard to separate the message from the messenger. But the instrumental products of our culture—these gorgeous sleek toys—do seem to turn everyone into objectified data, indifferent or immune to our status as persons with lives beyond Facebook communities, instant replays or replies. How might we inhabit this other world, unrecorded and unobserved? Do we cease to exist when we are here, in the actuality of a physical elsewhere? My young friend Andrew's message on his cell phone says, "I am not here" but *here* has no location in real timespace.

INCREASINGLY, I AM AWARE that what I have chosen to do or to be in my life is of decreasing relevance to the ways in which we think the world. Poetry, particularly contemporary written poetry of an experimental bent, has been dropped from the considerations of nearly all media outlets and is rarely referred to in our conversations. It has, of course, found ample refuge in the promiscuous animations of the Internet, in blogs and websites both useful and influential, at least to poets and students of poetry. As Ubuwebmeister Kenneth Goldsmith is said to have remarked, "If it isn't on the Internet it doesn't exist." This is not an uninteresting statement, connecting the neutral pronoun "it" to the idea of "existence" or rather non-existence. We have heard this word "it" before, in the objectification by our soldiers of their prisoners, at Abu Ghraib. Persons can easily become its.

POEMS ARE STRUCTURES that specifically resist the objectification of persons and the instrumentality of language. Many people think poems are little dressed up narratives of self-reflection, expressivity and catharsis, and indeed, many of them are. In a world that offers an endless glut of glittery selves that rise and fall through the limitless ether like Milton's angels, it is not difficult to understand why poetry has become anathema in the public imagination: it neither fully informs nor fully entertains. The best poems ride along the edge of relation where consciousness forms, opening the subject into the myriad predicates that constitute it. As cultural theorists, contemporary poets and philosophers have told us *ad infinitum*, the grammatical shifter "I" is not synonymous with a self, and a self cannot be either fully revealed or discovered in language. I once heard John Ashbery remark: "I am John. Ashbery writes the poems."

AS WE POETS TEETER ON THE VERGE OF EXTINCTION, we might find comfort in the words of Giorgio Agamben: "Those who are truly contemporary, who truly belong to their time, are those who neither perfectly coincide with it nor adjust themselves to its demands. They are thus in this sense irrelevant (*inattuale*)."[10]

GEORGE OPPEN'S GREAT POEM, "Of Being Numerous,"[11] from 1968, is among other things a meditation on the notion of the individual, the one. Oppen is exemplary for many of us, partly because he stopped writing poetry for twenty years in the face of an urgent politics, which he did not think poetry should or could address. He was included in the group called The Objectivists and had no truck with the augmented expressivity commonly associated, then as now, with poetry. His abiding value was clarity, *clarity*, as he wrote, *in the sense of silence*. I understand this form of silence, like that of John Cage, to be a trope for receptivity: for listening and waiting.

Here are some lines from his poem:

6
We are pressed, pressed on each other,
We will be told at once
Of anything that happens

And the discovery of fact bursts
In a paroxysm of emotion
Now as always. Crusoe

We say was
'Rescued'.
So we have chosen.

7
Obsessed, bewildered

By the shipwreck

Of the singular

We have chosen the meaning
Of being numerous.

FOR OPPEN, THE URBAN CROWD flowing through the city displaces the solitary "meditative man," the instant relay of event unleashes a "paroxysm of emotion," and the "mineral fact" of the material world accompanied by what he calls "the intensity of seeing" contribute to the "bright light of shipwreck." The urban did not hold for him the delectable anonymity of the flâneur, nor the insouciant serendipities that Frank O'Hara celebrates, nor the dystopic enclave of production of Warhol's factory. The upsurge of experimental freedoms of the 1960s appeared to Oppen as ominous.

The poem, here breaking into prose, continues:

10
Or, in that light, New arts! Dithyrambic, audience as artists! But
I will listen to a man, I will listen to a man, and when I speak I
will speak, tho he will fail and I will fail. But I will listen to him

speak. The shuffling of a crowd is nothing—well, nothing but the men that we are, but nothing.

Urban art, art of the cities, art of the young in the cities—the isolated man is dead, his world around him exhausted

And he fails! He fails, that meditative man! And indeed they cannot 'bear' it.

AND INDEED, WE CANNOT BEAR IT. Oppen anticipates the erosion of inwardness, not as self-absorption or narcissism, but as the receptivity necessary to thoughtfulness. He could not have known that thought would be consigned to opinion, or to the reclusive preference of brilliant eccentrics like J.D. Salinger. He could not have predicted that our thoughtful President would be vilified for lacking the aggressive temperament we have come to mistake for leadership.

OPPEN'S IMAGE of the bright light of shipwreck conjures for me all the untoward suddenness of our times: bombs exploding, towers falling, earthquakes rupturing: the flash of annihilation that hovers just on the other side of our earthly existence, and over which we have no say. For my generation, this hovering extinction was a given, felt as immanent threat from an implacable monolithic Other abstractly framed—it *was* an it, disassociated from persons; for this generation, the threat finds itself secreted, both intimate and diffuse, tucked inside cars and trucks and the undergarments of individuals whose care for this life, her life, his life, your life, my life, has been forfeited. This indifference to earthly life speaks into the absolute negative, where nothing is given in the here and now, and where the idea of choice presents itself as numbing obedience and renunciation. Our culture of "getting and spending," in Wordsworth's famous phrase, offers no appeal, our rhetoric of freedom falls on deaf ears.

BUT FOR THIS, our present moment, images of an apocalyptic catastrophe seem overly theatrical. What threaten are far subtler forms of destruction, inflicted from within: erosion, recalcitrance, redundancy, inertia, expedience, literalism, impatience, fraud, abuse. What threatens is a world of ostensible choice staged in an infinite regress of mirrors, unmoored from either historical contingency or consequence; a world of viral proliferation without difference. It is as if modernity's signal value, the new, had reformulated itself as tractionless spin, where everyone is simultaneously present and absent in an eviscerated but engorged "now" where nothing of actual consequence can happen.

ANN HAMILTON[12] SENT ME A BOOK called *Radical Hope: Ethics in the Face of Cultural Devastation.* The author, Jonathan Lear, considers the fate of the Crow nation, specifically through the life of Plenty Coups, their last great chief. Plenty Coups straddled the world between cultural vitality and cultural extinction, living to tell his story and the story of his people to a white interlocutor. Lear is struck by the fact that Plenty Coups refused to talk about anything after the Crow were confined to the reservation and the buffalo herd was eradicated. He said, "But when the buffalo went away the hearts of my people fell to the ground. And they could not lift them up again. After this nothing happened."

"AFTER THIS, NOTHING HAPPENED." For the Crow, history did indeed come to an end; all that they had lived for and believed in had vanished. Lear wonders what it might mean to have the concepts—the givens—that make it possible to understand oneself go out of existence, concepts which inform, as he puts it, "the intimate connection between thinking and being." He writes, "As it turns out, intending and hoping and wondering and desiring are not just up to me: they are not just a matter of exercising my will. And my ability to do so is not just a psychological issue: it is a question of the field in which psychological states are possible."[13]

THE IMAGE OF A FIELD is of course iconic in the American imagination; it is probably not an accident that Lear evokes it here. The field extends into familiar tropes— weavings, meadows, waves—which inflect countless novels, photographs; films, poems and paintings. The field informs our idealistic sense of the interplay between the one and the many, sameness and difference; our dream of mobility in the elastic lens between distant horizon and garden gate. Iterations and images of fields can be found in Whitman and Pollock, in Ann Hamilton and Agnes Martin, in Charles Olson and Robert Duncan, Maya Lin and James Schuyler. Schuyler wrote, "Past is past. I salute that various field." The image evokes the agrarian romance of the farm, the killing fields of war, the mute graves of the dead and the vibrant play of games; it announces the distinctive limit of the chosen; we have, we say, a field of interest. The field reminds us of the particular attachment we have to place, how that attachment has informed the geography of the mind.

THE CROW LOST THEIR FIELD OF VISION. What would it mean for their victorious enemy, ourselves, to lose ours, and who among us has the wisdom of Plenty Coups to know when nothing has happened?

I HAVE A COLLECTION of small works, paintings and drawings and sculptures, most of them gifts from friends and students. Like my books, I think of these objects as providing mute but tangible company. The pleasure I take from them is derived not only from their surface charms; each of them has within itself a temporal history of choices and decisions that is at once tacit and evident. My sense is that our love for certain artists and writers is bound up in our capacity to know or read this active field of engagement, of call and response; ways of distinguishing; turns of mind, indeed, to experience or inhabit the very moments of choice. I am not referring here merely to stylistic revelations of suturing or gesture, but rather to a more subtle kind of immanent unraveling of the motions of composition. Works of art restructure the present, anchoring it to the ground of an embodied materiality that has within itself the history of its making.

GERHARD RICHTER, *NOTES*, 1990:[14]

Accept that I can plan nothing. Any thoughts on my part about the 'construction' of a picture are false, and if the execution works, this is only because I partly destroy it, or because it works in spite of everything—by not detracting and by not looking the way I had planned. I often find this intolerable and even impossible to accept, because, as a thinking, planning human being, it humiliates me to find out that I am so powerless. It casts doubts on my competence and constructive ability. My only consolation is to tell myself that I did actually make the pictures—even though they are a law unto themselves, even though they treat me any way they like and somehow just take shape. Because it is still up to me to determine at what point they are finished (picture-making consists of a multitude of yes/ no decisions, with a Yes to end it all). If I look at it that way, the whole thing starts to seem quite natural again—or rather Nature like, alive—and the same thing applies to the comparison on the social level.

PHOTOGRAPHER JEFF WALL, IN AN INTERVIEW:[15]

When I started to work with the computer, I had the idea that I could use the otherworldly "special effects" to develop a kind of philosophical comedy...This makes me think of Diderot, of the idea that a certain light shone on behavior, costume, and discourse creates an amusement which helps to detach you from the immediate surroundings and projects you into a field of reflection in which humanity appears as infinitely imperfectible. This imperfection implies gentleness and forgiveness, and the artistic challenge is to express that without sentimentality.

Wall continues,

I guess the key metaphor in these works is "learning." We learn; we never complete the process of learning, and so learning is a kind of image of incompleteness and limitation, but a hopeful image as well."

He says that in one of his works, "The Stumbling Block,"

I thought I could imagine a further extrapolation of society in which therapy had evolved to a new, maybe higher stage...In my fantasy, The Stumbling Block helps people change. He is there so that ambivalent people can express their ambivalence by interrupting themselves in their habitual activities.

MICHAEL BRENSON, "THE LOOK OF THE ARTIST," 2010:[16]

My hunch is that most writers, curators and critics who regularly ask themselves "What am I looking at?" don't hear the more reflexive and dissonant question. They don't hear the "I" as also a "you" or the "you" in the "I." I cannot detach "What am I looking at?" from "What are you looking at?" The latter establishes within me an awareness that even in the moments of intense concentration I'm a stranger to myself, or, rather, that there's a stranger in myself, or rather there's a crowd in me, each member of which has had and still seems to want some voice in my perceiving and thinking. "What am I looking at?" gives me the feeling of being welcome to exchange territories in an encounter whose potential cost to me is moderated by a process of reciprocity and transition. "What are you looking at?" asserts the shock and risk, the challenge to process, of another experience of looking, one in which I do not know who is holding the cards and whether there is even the possibility of a conversation. The question establishes the existence in me of a vast psychological, sociological, political, and linguistic network.

TAKEN TOGETHER, THESE THREE QUOTATIONS begin to suggest the kinds of interactions that inhere in our experiences of art, whether as creators, readers, critics, or observers. Each has entered a set of relations, in which subjective and objective realities—the self and the material world—seem to engage the possibility of radical morphological change. They seem to suggest that when a given subject finds its form, something is released. My rather prosaic name of this thing is content. Content subverts the easy see-through that imagines we are transparent to each other; content, the alignment of subject with form, shifts us simultaneously toward the other and away from ourselves, opening the space for the connective tissue of meaning to be made.

IN HIS FINAL WORK, *PURE IMMANENCE: ESSAYS ON A LIFE*,[17]

Deleuze wrote:

But we shouldn't enclose life in the single moment when individual life confronts universal death. A life is everywhere, in all the moments that a given living subject goes through and that are measured by given lived objects: an immanent life carrying with it the events or singularities that are merely actualized in subjects and objects. This indefinite life does not itself have moments, close as they may be one to another, but only between-times, between moments; it doesn't just come about or come after but offers the immensity of an empty time where one sees the event yet to come already happened, in the absolute of an immediate consciousness.

THIS EVOCATION of a kind of molecular paradise of incipience, out of which certain objects and subjects precipitate, converting what is potential into the actuality of immediate consciousness, captures some of what I am trying to evoke. The plane of immanence reminds me of Agamben's notion of the "moment of arising" which "is objective and subjective at the same time…never the emergence of the fact without at the same time being the emergence of the knowing subject itself." I want to attach

Agamben's notion of a moment of arising and Deleuze's notion of a plane of immanence to my sense of what it means to allow a work of art to alter the givens of a life. The figure of an alert receptivity—the knowing that we know rather than what we know—informs these abstruse and enigmatic ideas.

I WANT TO SUGGEST that works of art might embody both ideas. The moments of immanence that the artist experiences are collapsed into the work, to be revived or reimagined by the spectator when she enters its arena; Agamben's moment of arising, the undecidable threshold between object or fact and subject, captures the alteration between subjectivities and historical contingency that the work of art precipitates and fosters and confirms.

PERHAPS THE EXPERIENCE I am trying to name is simply what animates the conversion of information into knowledge, where what we know is attached to reality through beliefs as well as facts, where affective reasoning informs our choices, decisions and judgments. You may have noticed that this final term, judgment, has been left out of my talk, It seems evident that we are living in a time of nearly continuous judgment, with little connection to the deliberative preludes entailed in choice and decision. Works of art stop before judgment occurs; they invite us to enlarge our capacity to integrate, absorb, and interpret; they may, as well, show us how to resist or refrain, in the words of Melville's Bartelby, to prefer not to. Works of art pivot and oscillate, activating our subjective sets, the givens that belong to both maker and recipient, causing them to relax their grip, release their boundaries, finally to risk autonomy in the face of alterity.

I WANT TO END BY TURNING to one of my most enduring companions in thought, Emerson,[18] and to his great essay "Experience," from 1843.

WHERE DO WE FIND OURSELVES? He begins. He does not ask, where do I find myself, although the central underlying event of the essay is the death of his young son Waldo. Emerson begins in a state of paralytic denial, in which he says that the loss of his son has had no impact, has changed nothing: I grieve that I cannot grieve, he writes. Emerson begins his essay in what Emily Dickinson called *the hour of lead*. As he writes, the essay—which I think of as a prose poem—takes on a kind of animation, breathing and exhaling at an almost impossibly slow pace. It meanders and it dwells. The sense of wandering makes it impossible to capture or to paraphrase; I cannot ever recall what it says, although I have read it dozens of times. The sense one has is that one is undergoing something, of being drawn through a constellation of emerging and disappearing tropes and topics. This attenuated and circuitous journey, this ingathering, pivots for Emerson around the fact of subjective consciousness: "It is very unhappy, but too late to be helped, the discovery we have made, that we exist." Knowledge that we exist brings forth knowledge that we shall cease to exist: "Nothing left us now but death," he writes. Indeed, there is nothing in the material world that is not elusive and slippery. "I take this evanescence and lubricity of all objects, which lets them slip through our fingers when we clutch hardest, to be the most unhandsome part of our condition." At every turn, we sense the abiding fact of the death of Waldo. And yet, slowly, phrase-by-phrase, the writing begins to alter its webs of negative intransigence.

IT ENDS: "Never mind the ridicule, never mind the

defeat: up again, old heart! It seems to say—there is victory yet for all justice; and the true romance which the world exists to realize, will be the transformation of genius into practical power."

FOR EMERSON, experience, the experience of writing the essay called experience, results in the transformation of genius into practical power. His deadened, inert heart comes back to life. Genius, the given, finds the will to animate the recalcitrant and obdurate into new forms of "practical power." The shut world opens out, the given and the chosen greet and touch across the threshold.

NOTES

[1] At the invitation of David Levi Strauss, Chair of Art Criticism and Writing at the School of Visual Arts in Manhattan, I first gave this talk as part of his Lecture Series on the 11th of February 2010. Subsequently, I gave it for the Writers' Caucus at Bard's Milton Avery Graduate School of the Arts in the summer of 2010, and again for the Sculpture Department at Yale School of the Arts in New Haven, Connecticut in the spring of 2011.

[2] This passage comes at the end of Canto VI in the section called "It Must Give Pleasure." The poem is from Stevens' fifth collection, *Transport to Summer* (1947).

[3] Marcel Mauss, *Essai sur le don*, first published in 1923. Lewis Hyde's *The Gift: Imagination and the Erotic Life of Property* was first published in 1979.

[4] Sometimes I wonder how much real influence these astonishing thinkers have had; influence on the Real. How does thought change

action? It is an old question, one I certainly cannot answer, except to go on hoping that it can and does alter how we go on going on. In any case, this comment on Foucault by Gilles Deleuze can be found in *Negotiations 1972–1990*, translated by Martin Joughin (New York, Columbia University Press, 1995) p.96.

[5] My colleague at Bard, Joan Retallack, has written eloquently on John Cage. Her book *The Poethical Wager* (Berkeley, The University of California Press, 2003) has an insightful essay on Cage, "Poethics of a Complex Realism." My own sense of him is in part based on having met him, with Merce Cunningham, on my thirtieth birthday, in London, at the house of John Russell and Suzi Gablik, and subsequently, or perhaps prior to that, in Cadaques, Spain, where he had visited with Duchamp and with Duchamp's widow, Teeny, and their friend, the English artist Richard Hamilton. Being in the presence of John Cage was a source of continuous enlightenment. Happily, he continues to be present in his music and writings.

[6] To be exact: 142 East 18th Street, between Irving Place and Third Avenue, when the El still rumbled along, and Gramercy Park was still the provenance of the super privileged. The building, dubbed "the second oldest apartment building in New York" had been built by the family of Peter Stuyvesant, and was known as "Stuyvesant's Folly," since the idea of an apartment building was at the time of its erecting an anathema to brownstone Manhattan. It had two wings,

a large lobby with a courtyard beyond, mahogany staircases, and long, seven-room apartments with working fireplaces. The building attracted artists and intellectuals; among them, Louise Bourgeois and her husband, the art critic Robert Goldwater. Their sons, Jean-Louis and Alain, were childhood friends, and visits to their apartment, in the opposite wing, were perhaps my first glimpse of another cultural reality. The building was torn down in the late 1950s to make room for a more profitable yellow brick misery.

[7] Georg Simmel, *On Individuality and Social Forms*. Edited and translated by Donald N. Levine. (Chicago, The University of Chicago Press. 1971) p. 230. Italics his. The quotation is taken from a chapter called "Subjective Culture."

[8] Jaron Lanier, *You Are Not a Gadget: A Manifesto* (New York, Alfred A. Knopf, 2010). Lanier has continued to advocate a contrarian position with intelligence and wit. A profile of him by Jennifer Kahn, "The Visionary," appeared in *The New Yorker* July 11 & 18, 2011. When I went to buy his book at Barnes and Noble shortly after it was published, I had to search for it and finally found it on a back table.

[9] Jose Ortega Y Gasset, *The Dehumanization of Art* (Princeton, Princeton University Press, 1948). Parts were reprinted in *The Idea of the Modern in Literature and the Arts* (New York, Horizon Press, 1967), edited by Irvng Howe. This collection is instructive in its

selection of ideas (futurism, symbolism, surrealism, dada) and figures (Baudelaire by Sartre, Proust by Martin Turnell, Thomas Mann and Andre Gide by Kenneth Burke. Rilke and Nietzsche by Erich Heller, T.S. Eliot by Delmore Schwartz, Wallace Stevens by J.V. Cunningham, Yeats by Conor Cruise O'Brien). There is an essay by Paul Goodman on American "advance-guard" writing, 1900–1950, which mentions no American writers, and another by Harold Rosenberg, "Aesthetics of Crisis" on the now almost entirely forgotten British painter and writer David Jones. The book includes "A Manifesto of Italian Futurism." As late as 1967, the American intellectual/artistic community was still looking almost entirely toward Europe for clues. Howe's group portrait of "the idea of the modern" perhaps sheds light on why Black Mountain College, which was founded in 1933 and closed in 1957, has continued to be perceived as a definitive generative institution for experimental artistic practice and thought in America, drawing its initial inspiration not from Europe but from the progressive pragmatism of John Dewey. Dewey's paradigmatic nexus of art, experience, and nature as essential to democratic pedagogical ideals seems more relevant now than ever.

[10] In Giorgio Agamben, *What is an Apparatus? And Other Essays.* Translated by David Kishik and Stefan Pedatella. (Stanford, Stanford University Press, 2009), p.40. The quotation is from the essay "What is the Contemporary?" (A question that seems to be on many minds, as we ditch the cumbersome epithet postmodern.) In

this passage, Agamben quotes Roland Barthes' citing Nietzsche, "The contemporary is the untimely." Agamben elaborates: "Those who coincide too well with the epoch, those who are perfectly tied to it in every respect, are not contemporaries, precisely because they do not manage to see it; they are not able to firmly hold their gaze on it." This seems useful, not just as a flourish of counter-intuition. It suggests that it is important to think of the present not as the last of a linear or serial sequence indebted to "newness", but as a constantly shifting set that cannot be steadied into any particular temporal or spatial, aesthetic or political Real. The present is a shape-shifter, endowed with innumerable possible ways of seeing, knowing, being. But the merely multifarious is not sufficient. Agamben says we need to pay attention to the obscure, the darkness. Here he echoes the French novelist Georges Perec's perhaps more compelling desire to "describe what remains: that which we generally don't notice, which doesn't call attention to itself, which is of no importance; what happens when nothing happens, what passes when nothing passes, except time, people, car, and clouds." This in turn reminds me of Anselm Berrigan's marvelous book, *Notes from Irrelevance* (Wave Books, 2011).

[11] All quotes are from George Oppen, *The Collected Poems of George Oppen* (New York, New Directions, 1975). The founder and publisher of New Directions, James Laughlin, sent this book, a first edition, to me after I wrote to him, desperately trying to find a copy. Laughlin said in his

note to me that it was his last copy. The poem "Of Being Numerous" was published in Oppen's eponymous fourth book, which, amazingly, won the Pulitzer Prize for 1968. The times they were a' changing.

[12] Ann Hamilton and I have had a conversation over many years. We share in a resistance to wholesale negativity in the face of the chronic thwart to hopes for a more equitable and joyous world. She is a person of apparently unlimited perseverance and courage; her work inevitably reaches, for me, the crux of the matter. Furthermore, technology is always in service to her vision of a fully embodied art.

[13] Jonathan Lear, *Radical Hope: Ethics in the Face of Cultural Devastation* (Cambridge, Harvard University Press, 2006). Lear's book is a kind of morality tale, in which "radical hope" appears through the ability to accept profound changes while maintaining a central core of value. In the case of Plenty Coups, this capacity came through a dream of the habits of the chickadee, and what Lear here calls, via Aristotle, "the critique of abysmal reasoning."

[14] In Gerhard Richter, *The Daily Practice of Painting: Writings 1962–1993*. Hans-Ulrich Obrist, editor; David Britt, translator. Cambridge, the MIT Press, 1995). David Britt translated these early Richter writings. David and I shared an office at Thames and Hudson publishers on Bloomsbury Street in London when we were both very young. He was knowledgeable and meticulous; we became friends, despite the

fact that I was comparatively ignorant and woefully inconsistent, not good traits in an editor. He died some years ago.

[15] The interview is with Arielle Pelene, and is included in *Jeff Wall: Selected Essays and Interviews* (New York, The Museum of Modern Art, 2007). There is a passage in the beginning of this interview that I like as much as, possibly more than, the one I quote. Wall says, "In the aesthetic of art photography as it was inspired by photojournalism, the image is clearly a fragment of a greater whole which itself can never be experienced directly. The fragment then, somehow, makes that whole visible or comprehensible, maybe through a complex typology of gestures, objects, moods, and so on. But, there is an 'outside' to the picture, and that outside weighs down on the picture, demanding significance from it. The rest of the world remains unseen, but present, with its demand to be expressed or signified in, or as, a fragment of itself."

[16] The essay from which this is taken, "The Look of the Artist", is included in *Learning Mind: Experience into Art*, edited by Mary Jane Jacob and Jacquelynn Baas (Berkeley, The University of California Press, 2010). This meditation comes after a series of questions Brenson asks, beginning with "What are you looking at?" which the sculptor Juan Munoz said, in 1996, was "his first artistic question."

[17] Gilles Deleuze, *Pure Immanence: Essays on A Life*. Translated by Anne Boyman. (New York, Zone Books, 2005). Deleuze begins this book with a question, "What is a transcendental field?" His answer, "It can be distinguished from experience in that it doesn't refer to an object or belong to a subject (empirical representation). It appears therefore as a pure stream of a-subjective consciousness, a pre-reflexive impersonal consciousness, a qualitative duration of consciousness without a self." This assertion of an "it" invites the most radical speculation. Aside from the obvious referent— God— it suggests the massive database of, say, Google, or perhaps more ominously, Ray Kurzweil's Singularity.

[18] Ralph Waldo Emerson (1803–1882). His essays are widely available, from Penguin Classics and from the Library of America. I like to think that anyone who cares about thinking about being a thinking being has read Emerson. He wrestled with some central ideas of modernity, attaching the saturated field of European thought to a desire for a particularly American intellectual bearing. Stanley Cavell has written widely on Emerson. See also Joan Richardson's A *Natural History of Pragmatism: The Fact of Feeling from Jonathan Edwards to Gertrude Stein*, from Cambridge University Press, 2007, and Richard Deming's *Listening on All Sides: Toward an Emersonian Ethics of Reading*, from Stanford University Press, 2007.

PHOTO BY MARINA VAN ZUYLEN

Ann Lauterbach is the author of eight books of poetry, several collaborations with visual artists, and an essay collection, *The Night Sky: Writings on the Poetics of Experience*. Her most recent book, *Or to Begin Again* (2009) was a finalist for a National Book Award. She is Ruth and David Schwab Professor of Languages and Literature at Bard College, where she is also co-director of Writing in the Milton Avery Graduate School of the Arts, and is a core critic in the Yale School of Art (Sculpture). Among her awards are a Guggenheim Fellowship and a MacArthur Fellowship. She lives in Germantown, New York.